CONSTANTLY WONDERING IF YOU ARE MAKING THE BIGGEST MISTAKE OF YOUR LIFE

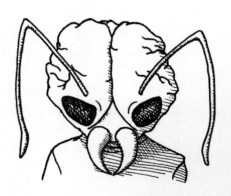

ILLUSTRATED BY SARAH MILLER

LOVE IS NOT CONSTANTLY WONDERING IF YOU
ARE MAKING THE BIGGEST MISTAKE OF YOUR LIFE
4th printing December 2014

Artist: Sarah Miller

All rights reserved.
Choose Your Own Adventure is a registered
trademark of Chooseco, LLC and is used here without
their permission

Copyright © 2011 by the author
This book may not be reproduced, in whole or in part, by
mimeograph or by any other means, without permission.
For information contact: bunnyproject@gmail.com
or visit www.perfectdaypublishing.com

Published in Portland, Oregon in association with
Perfect Day Publishing.

ISBN 978-0-9836327-2-6

PRINTED IN THE UNITED STATES OF AMERICA

LOVE IS NOT
CONSTANTLY
WONDERING IF
YOU ARE MAKING
THE BIGGEST
MISTAKE OF YOUR
LIFE

Warning!!!!!

You can read this book straight through from beginning to end if you want to. These pages contain one adventure about the time you, a guy who does not care for drinking, dated an alcoholic. It is also about crashing on a planet of giant malevolent space ants. From time to time as you read along you will be asked to make a choice. Your choice will have no meaningful impact on anything that happens. So this will all make a lot more sense if you just read it from beginning to end.

August 1, 2002

It is a beautiful day. You walk up the stairs to the library. There is a girl sitting on the steps, smoking. She is pretty in a Virginia-Woolf-meets-Helena-Bonham-Carter-in-Fight-Club sort of way. You exchange, "I think you look interesting but I'll be damned if I'm going to make the first move" glances, then pull the doors open and step inside.

While looking at movies you see her staring at you. And again while flipping through a pile of graphic novels. Every time you look up, she looks away. Every time she looks up, you look away. You find excuses not to leave, browsing through sections that hold no interest to you in order to prolong your opportunity to steal glances. Eventually you decide that this is getting ridiculous and you walk up to her and introduce yourself. Here is what you find out:

- Her name is Anne.
- She is 22 years old.
- She just moved here from North Carolina.
- She plays the cello.
- She is a stripper.

Regarding this last piece of information, you have a great idea. You will make a joke about how you are a sperm donor and you both make money from your bodies. But you are having trouble figuring out exactly how to phrase it, and now like ten seconds have passed and you still haven't said anything and you are worried that she will think that you are freaked out that she is a stripper. In

August 1, 2002

the end you have fifteen seconds of awkward silence, followed by you even more awkwardly explaining why you didn't say anything. Despite you being a huge dork she seems amused. You ask her for her e-mail address and she gives it to you.

Turn to August 8, 2002

August 6, 2002

You are at the coffee shop with Anne. It is your first date. She orders a quadruple espresso poured into a cup half full with cold water. She drains it in one gulp. You are simultaneously disgusted and aroused.

You talk about yourself, she talks about herself. You go through all the standard first date getting-to-know-each-other questions. She is fascinating, not necessarily for her answers, but for how she talks. It is all riddle and allusion and metaphor. Listening to her is like trying to decipher an unholy amalgam of Tori Amos and Muhammad Ali.

You like her. You're probably too different for this not to explode into a fiery mess after a few weeks, but you like her.

Turn to November 19, 2003

August 8, 2002

This is your first kiss with Anne, and it is probably the most memorable first kiss of your life. She mentioned that she had never seen a shooting star, so you lay on the roof of her apartment building with her, watching the Perseids. After, she walked you back to where you locked your bike and the two of you sat on the curb, talking. It was chilly for August and you sat pressing your sides together, greedy for the other's heat. Eventually, a pause in conversation. You look at her. She looks at you. You kiss. It is utterly magical for about five

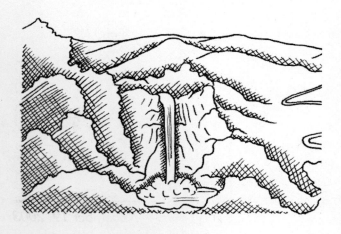

August 8, 2002

seconds, right up until the point where the drunk guy stumbles out of the bar and starts pissing on the wall next to you.

If you decide to do a crash landing in the alien jungle below, turn to October 25, 2002

If you decide you would rather take your chances with ejecting from your X-37 Spacefighter, turn to the next page

August 21, 2002

You are at the Flaming Lips/Beck concert and Anne is drunk. Not super drunk. But drunk enough that she has decided that you both need to go backstage, and drunk enough that she thinks telling the bouncer, "We are supposed to be backstage," will work. And definitely drunk enough that when the bouncer responds, "No you're not," she is unable to think of a response other than running away.

You walk back to her car and she says she is not ready to drive yet. She is parked on the top of a parking garage and the two of you lie on the hood of her car and talk about the show while the rest of the lot empties. It is a beautiful night, and warm, and once the rest of the cars leave you decide to enjoy some brisk post-concert makeouts. You are having a lovely time when all those beers catch up to Anne and the urge to pee hits her like a freight train.

She decides there is no time to find a bathroom, hikes up her skirt, and squats down behind the car. You didn't realize until now how much Anne had to drink. She has been peeing for what seems like at least a minute when you decide to start timing her. From this moment until she finishes will be two minutes. She mourns that there isn't someone from Guinness here to witness this. The thing is... when you pee for three minutes, it results in a lot of pee. It's not long before Anne is completely surrounded. The other thing is, while Anne can pee for three minutes, she can only keep her balance while squatting for about two and a half.

August 21, 2002

This is the story of the time you left your underpants in Syracuse because Anne needed them to clean herself after she fell into her puddle of urine.

Turn to September 14, 2006

September 10, 2002

You are bored so you decide to give Anne a call. She answers. You ask her what she is doing. She replies, "My roommate".

Which is weird. Not because it's a surprise at all. You know that they fooled around. You and Anne have talked about it. You know that her roommate has a fiance down in North Carolina and he has no problem with the two of them together. They have been doing this off-and-on for years. And you didn't really feel like it was your place to object. After all, she was there first. She is not the one stealing Anne, you are. But it catches you off-guard. You spend forty hours a week minimum playing video games and Dungeons and Dragons. By all rights you should be living in your mom's basement. It is weird what your problems have become.

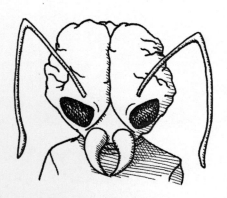

Turn to August 8, 2003

October 13, 2002

You follow Anne up the stairs to your bedroom but she closes the door behind her. You knock and say you want to talk to her. She replies that she doesn't want to talk, and you can tell from the slur in speech that she is drunk again. It is strange to be around her when she has been drinking. She is like the evil version of Spock, the one with the sash and the goatee. She looks like herself, and sort of acts like herself, but there is something else inside her. She is mean when she drinks, and bellicose, and you have told her you don't like being around her when she is like this.

When you first started dating Anne didn't drink at all. After a few weeks she started coming home from work drunk. It would get progressively worse until she would have a really bad night, lose her shit, and promise that she would get sober. She would be fine for a few days, then she would be at a concert or something and decide that yeah, she can have one drink. She has her one, and decides that because she was able to stop at one then she can probably control her drinking at work now. So she starts drinking at work again....

You are grateful that she seems to have things relatively under control. You are grateful that it is only alcohol, and not something harder that could cause real problems.

If you want to try to communicate with the giant, mutated ant, turn to August 6, 2002

If you want to examine it, turn to August 21, 2005

October 25, 2002

You are in the waiting room of Planned Parenthood and you are scared out of your mind. Anne is getting back the results of her HIV test. You knew that it would take a long time. There is a lengthy spiel that they go through before they give you the results, regardless of how things turn out. But you have been here for an hour. It should not have taken this long. You think about how careless the two of you have been. You have always used a condom during sex, but there has often been sort of a grey area between "sex" and "genitals get slightly inserted into other genitals during foreplay." And right now that grey area is in the back of your head screaming, "HOLY FUCK DUDE WE ARE GOING TO DIE OF AIDS."

Eventually a somber looking nurse shuffles over to where you are sitting. "We need to see you in the back." You try to stand as your stomach drops through the floor. You follow the nurse. One foot in front of the other until she opens a door to an examination room. Anne is lying on the table with her eyes closed. The doctor turns to you and smiles. "Oh, hi! Sorry about the wait. We lost the results of Anne's last test. We took some more blood, but then she got woozy and needed to lie down, and we thought you might have been tired of sitting out there by yourself."

NEVER AGAIN. Never again will you walk the slippery slope of "genitals get slightly inserted into other genitals."

Turn to January 24, 2004

November 13, 2002

Today is your twenty-fourth birthday. Your friends are throwing you a party. Anne shows up late. And drunk. And belligerent. And when you beat her at air hockey she takes off her shoe and whips it at your head.

You always knew there would be consequences to dating someone who considers Courtney Love to be her role model. In theory it seemed great. All excitement and adventure and fuck yous. Which, some of the time, it is. But you think about tonight, and how embarrassed you feel to have this happen in front of your friends. And all you can see is a future of her showing up trashed for your daughter's sweet sixteen party and musical collaborations with Billy Corgan and probably a lot of somehow even worse things that you can't even imagine.

Turn to August 8, 2002

November 26, 2002

Anne leaves tomorrow morning to spend the week with her family in North Carolina. Her roommate is out of town so you head over to their place. Anne has bronchitis, and when you arrive she is messed up on cold medicine (or at least her version of cold medicine, which is a can of Diet Coke mixed with a much larger bottle of Bacardi). It feels silly to be upset about this when she is only going to be gone for a week, but staying up with her till dawn watching her oscillate between giggling and crying was not the send-off you had hoped for. You know that drinking is what normal people do, and you are a weirdo in that regard, but you can't help but feel that alcohol has been getting in the way of a lot of what are supposed to be special occasions lately.

Turn to February 12, 2005

December 7, 2002

"I really don't want this. I like having a crazy, frenetic girlfriend. Not a crazy, alcohol-abusing girlfriend. It's gotten to the point where she needs to clean up, or I'm going to have to end it."

These words are going to be a recurring theme over the course of the next four years. You are Leia, and she is Han Solo, and those words are your, "I have a bad feeling about this."

If you hide by diving into the garbage pit, turn to September 27, 2004

If you decide to hold the Ant Warriors off by firing at them with your blaster, turn to July 12, 2005

December 19, 2002

It is one thing for her to show up at your house trashed, lock herself in the bathroom, and throw apples against the wall until the tiles break. Or for her to almost get pulled out of her car for threatening to run over some woman's kid. You can deal with stuff like that just fine. You don't want to, but you can. However, to be so drunk that she goes to the wrong movie theatre, and as a result you and your friends end up missing the midnight premiere of *The Two Towers* because you made them wait for her? That is not fucking acceptable.

Turn to March 10, 2004

January 20, 2003

Things have been better lately. You talked to Anne, apologized for being in such a bad mood. Told her that it can be draining being around her when she is drunk. You can handle the little things, but when she gets violent or self-destructive, right now you have nothing left in you to cope with that. Anne agreed to take better care of herself, and to try to not be around you when she is drinking.

Now you are on top of a parking garage. It is warm today, and Anne is sober, and you bought two hundred bouncy balls to have a contest to see who can throw them the farthest. It feels like things are returning to normal, or at least whatever normal is for you and Anne.

Turn to March 30, 2003

March 2, 2003

You are going to be late. It was a given that you were going to be late. You just weren't sure how it would happen. It turns out the catalyst will be that Anne was wrong about how little gas there was in the car, so now the two of you are walking down the side of the highway, in a blizzard, carrying gas in big, broken-lidded cans that have splashed all over both of you.

There is never a question of whether something is going to go wrong when Anne is involved. It feels like the universe conspires against her. There was a time when making plans was easy. That time was before you met Anne. Now you not only consider the worst possible scenario, but also scenarios where Anne is attacked by bears, or her car is stolen, or that a simple traffic stop might end with her being charged as a terrorist. You do your best to predict these possibilities, to put yourself in a situation where you can mitigate as much of the damage as possible. But days like today are inevitably going to happen.

Turn to October 14, 2006

March 30, 2003

Anne has decided to apply to music school. It is about six hours away, at the northernmost tip of the state. You agree to come with her to the audition, and the trip there is an extended lesson in why driving with Anne is one of the most terrifying experiences in the world. There are electrical problems with her car, an old Chevy sedan that resembles a giant blue boat more than it does a car, and whenever the headlights are on, the open-door noise chimes incessantly. Which is why you are currently speeding up I-81 at about eighty miles an hour with the lights out. While flurries of snow blow the car all over the road. At night. And she is holding a cup of coffee and smoking a cigarette and is talking on a cell phone. The fact that she has never been in an accident makes it hard to decide if she is a very good driver or a very bad one.

The specter of imminent death hanging over the car ride provides a welcome distraction to thoughts of what will happen if Anne moves away.

Turn to October 18, 2003

May 12, 2003

Today is uncomfortable truths day. You think about *Fight Club*, and how all through the movie Marla's actions are crazy and incomprehensible. And then at the end you find out that she was not the one acting weird, she was just responding to the fact that Ed Norton had a split personality and in that moment you are forced to reevaluate who has been the asshole in the relationship. This is that moment for you.

You can tell yourself you are a good boyfriend all you want. You can pat yourself on the back for being so tolerant and understanding and patient with Anne's drinking. But the truth is you are cold and unemotional and distant when Anne needs to be close to you. And maybe you need to recognize the part you play in her unhappiness, and the part you play in her drinking. Maybe if you were willing to open your heart a little she wouldn't have to drink so much in the first place.

If you decide to stand firm and tell the interrogator that there are four lights, turn to April 12, 2005

If you decide to end the torture by lying and telling him there are five lights, turn to January 4, 2004

May 12, 2003

May 14, 2003

This is a trap. You know you are not a perfect boyfriend. You know it bothers her that you can be so guarded with your emotions. That when the two of you fight, and she is crying while your voice is flat and dead, it makes her question if you really care for her at all.

But she doesn't need your distance to make her unhappy. She is capable of being unhappy all by herself. You are not the reason she drinks. Keep telling yourself that. Hopefully one day you will believe it.

Turn to January 13, 2004

May 28, 2003

Anne bursts through the door in her typical fashion, with a grace that bespeaks a bull in a china shop if the bull was made of a thousand devastating tornadoes. You pause your game to watch her entrance, and she sheds coats and shirts and shoes and bags in a trail behind her as she crosses the room. She is glowing with excitement, and you ask her what's up.

She has been accepted at music school and has decided that she will definitely attend. You are happy for her. You talk about all the things that she will have to do before she leaves in August, and all the opportunities this will bring her. What you never discuss is what this means for the two of you. It is something you have thought about a lot since you went with her to visit the school, but you are afraid to broach the topic because you don't see how her moving six hours away can mean anything but breaking up.

If you try and dig through the cave-in to get to the trapped prisoners, turn to April 22, 2005

If you decide to leave the trapped behind in order to save the ones that are still with you, turn to March 10, 2004

June 29, 2003

Anne just left. A month in North Carolina with her family, then a few more weeks up here, then she is gone. You have no idea how you're going to do this. You still haven't talked about what will happen once she leaves. You don't want to break up, and you don't want to have a long distance relationship, and you don't see any other option. This unanswered question is slowly crushing you. It is a conversation with no happy outcome, and neither of you have the courage to bring it up.

Turn to October 30, 2006

August 8, 2003

You and Anne are in Toronto for the weekend. One last trip to remember things by. Anne loses her ID. You go to a Tori Amos concert. Her car gets towed. You walk for miles in the rain to the impound lot. You eat delicious food. When you are trying to cross back into the country the Border Agent is giving you a hard time and he searches the duffel bag where she keeps her work boots and is so overcome by the smell that he starts dry heaving. The weekend could not be a more perfect capping of your year together.

Turn to September 11, 2004

August 14, 2003

Anne is crying. You are in her apartment, in her bed, holding her in your arms. Today is her birthday. Tomorrow she leaves for school. You don't know when you will see her again, or what the status of things will be when you do. You run your fingers across the small of her back. You try to empty your mind of everything but the softness of her skin. You want to burn the memory of her into your brain while you still can. You drag your fingertips up her back, across her shoulder, down her arm. With your thumb and forefinger you make a circle around her wrist, measuring it. You bury your face in her neck. She tastes like sweat and nicotine. She smells like vanilla. You close your eyes. This is the edge of the world. You cannot imagine where you go from here.

If you follow the tunnel with the breeze that might lead back to the surface, turn to April 10, 2006

If you explore deeper and find out more about what the Ant-Warriors have hidden in their underground lair, turn to May 20, 2005

September 2, 2003

Anne is in town for the weekend. She is running out of money so she has come back to pick up a few shifts and pay her rent. Finally, finally, you sit down with her and try to figure out where things stand. Neither of you are really interested in a long-distance relationship. But she is going to need to come back every few weeks in order to work. And while that is definitely not what either of you want your relationship to look like, you both agree that until one of you meets someone new there really isn't a reason to break up.

The subtext of this conversation is that both of you want to get laid.

Turn to January 20, 2003

September 29, 2003

You are visiting Anne at school for the week. She leaves in the morning to go to class. You read, you play video games, you do all the cleaning that Anne hasn't gotten to in the month she's lived here. You have dinner ready when she comes home from school, and you spend the evening watching movies together. Yesterday was just like this. Tomorrow will be just like this. But it is nice. Maybe it has something to do with being able to play games for eight hours a day while a cat sits on your lap, but all this feels like playing house. It feels comfortable.

Turn to March 10, 2004

October 4, 2003

Anne is at a club with you and your roommate. Some douchebag in a mesh shirt comes up to your roommate and tells her that she is pretty. Anne responds, "Well, now isn't her life worth living." The douchebag calls Anne a bitch. Anne shoves the douchebag. The douchebag shoves Anne back. Anne tries to rip out the douchebag's nipple rings. This is the story of the second time Anne got banned from the club.

Three minutes later you and the roommate and your friends are trying to get Anne down the stairs and outside. The bouncers have you surrounded, and are taunting her, calling her a cunt, daring her to try and hit them. They are pretty mad at her, because the story of the first time Anne got banned from the club involved her fighting all the bouncers at once, and when they tried to pick her up to carry her out it just made it easier for her to kick them in the face. They are trying to goad her into throwing a punch so that they can have her arrested.

This is probably going to be the most exciting Saturday night you will ever experience.

Turn to December 8, 2005

October 18, 2003

It is three in the morning when the phone rings, and you answer to the sound of Anne sobbing hysterically. You can hear the sounds of a car. She says they are coming. She was at a party, and they are coming, and she is sorry. The line goes dead.

If you would like to use the radio to return the distress call, turn to October 7, 2006

If you would prefer to stare at the radio while being slowly overwhelmed by dread and longing and sadness, turn to September 11, 2004

October 19, 2003

Anne has been arrested for driving while intoxicated. She called you after the cop pulled her over, while he was walking from his car to hers. She needs to borrow five hundred dollars for a lawyer. You know that if you don't help her now, things will only be worse. You look at her life and the chaos that constantly surrounds her. She is drowning. She gives everything she has to keep her head above the water long enough to take that next breath. Maybe if you just give her a little boost, that will be the reprieve she needs so she can stop worrying only about survival. Maybe this is the push that will make things start to get better. You don't know it yet, but this is not true. This will never be true. This hope will help sustain you many times during your relationship, and it is never going to come to pass.

If you decide to make a break for it before more guards arrive, turn to September 20, 2005

If you decide to try and free the other prisoners first, turn to March 30, 2005

October 24, 2003

You are lying in bed when you hear Anne get in. Your roommate and her new boyfriend and her friends are having a party in the living room. This party is them drinking and acting obnoxious, and the first thing the boyfriend said when you met him was "You're not a fag, are you?" You have decided to go to bed early.

Anne spent the afternoon driving back from school and the evening working, and now she is here and you can tell by the sound of her voice that she is drunk. You push the disappointment out of your mind and close your eyes. Time slips away from you until suddenly Anne is standing over you laughing, holding a cup of water that she is dripping onto your wet face and now sleep is impossibly far away while something red and hostile floods in and fills the space behind your eyes. You have no words for her. You don't touch her you don't look at her just grab your shoes and a coat and walk out the door past your still drunk roommate and her asshole boyfriend and now you are walking down the street still in your bare feet.

How dare she. How fucking dare she. One week after she is arrested she is drinking and driving again. After she asked for your help so she could afford a lawyer, she comes into your house and spits in your face and shows you how little all the things you do really mean to her.

When you are a few blocks away you stop and put on your shoes. You walk until dawn trying to let go of the anger, but this is something

October 24, 2003

permanent. It is not going to fade in time and leave a scar. This is going to hobble you.

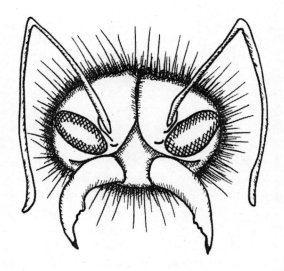

Turn to June 20, 2006

November 19, 2003

It would be inaccurate to say that you wake up lying across the front seat of Anne's car because that would imply that you had gotten any actual sleep. Saving money by spending the night in her car seemed like a good idea at the time, but you brought no blankets, no pillows. The experience was miserable. It is below freezing outside, and it feels barely warmer in the car.

You don't want to sit up. To sit up would be to admit defeat. You are exhausted and if you sit up it means you definitely aren't going to sleep anymore. But upon reflection, it is probably a lot more comfortable than continuing to lie here with the seat belts poking into you. With a grunt you pull yourself up. The windows are frosted over. The interior of the car is bathed in the soft yellow of the morning sun. You are in the parking lot of a Dunkin' Donuts and through the windows you can make out the blurry shadows of other cars. Anne is still asleep in the back. She looks beautiful in the light, and you sit for a while watching the puffs of cloud as she exhales.

You are very cold, and this feels like an adventure.

If you help the cavemen fight against the ants, turn to October 4, 2003

If you don't want to get involved and choose to flee back through the time vortex, turn to August 2, 2004

November 19, 2003

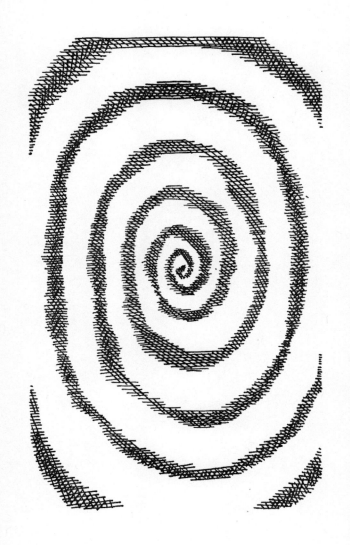

December 17, 2003

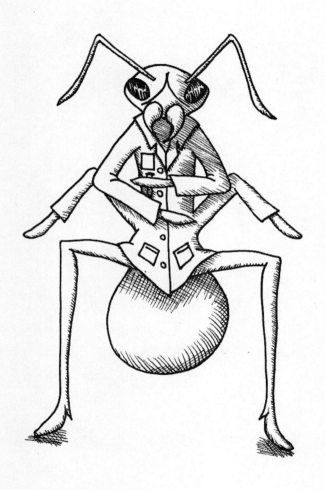

December 17, 2003

Anne is moving in. She will be in North Carolina for a few weeks with her family, and then she will join you and your roommate and your other roommate in an apartment that is not nearly big enough. Between the DUI and the legal fees and speeding tickets and only being able to work for a few days every couple of weeks, she can't afford to pay for school any more. She is still drinking. You have a bad feeling about this.

If you decide to trust the Ant-Scientist and drink the vial of strangely-glowing liquid, turn to August 7, 2006

If you decide to only pretend to drink it, and then spit it out when he isn't looking, turn to October 11, 2006

January 4, 2004

Anne is coming home tonight, and you've missed her, and it will be nice to see her again. But at the same time life is really fucked up in about five different ways right now. Somewhere in your head is a much longer version of this where you talk about addiction and the ache that is eating the left side of your skull and all you want to do is lie down and think about how it hurts and not do anything just think about that pain and what it means. But you are not quite there just yet.

Turn to February 12, 2004

January 13, 2004

It is three in the morning and Anne is drunk and naked and has one cigarette left. While the latter two of those qualities are absolutes, somehow her drunkenness is the most true of the three. You have spent the better part of an hour arguing about how she is not allowed to climb onto the six-inch icy ledge outside your window to smoke her last cigarette when she decides to try and force her way out. She is halfway outside before you pull her back in, and the cigarette breaks in the process. Up until now the argument was heated because of the alcohol, but the ridiculousness of her plan kept things from getting serious. But with the loss of her cigarette something in Anne snaps and she gets mean.

You are both screaming. Anne wants to go outside and walk around naked until she can find someone who will give her a smoke. You know she is saying it to try to hurt you. You let her implication pass and tell her she needs to lie down and sleep this off. She wants out. She tries to lunge past and you grab for her and Anne swings at your face. It connects and you feel nothing and before she can throw another you wrap your arms around her and trap her arms against her sides. You trip her legs and crash to the floor on top of her. She is screaming curses at you and struggling to break free, kicking and headbutting. You relax, letting your body turn to dead weight, pinning her against the floor.

Eventually her voice gives out. She stops struggling. The rage leaves her and the sorrow of

January 13, 2004

alcohol kicks in and you feel her body shake with sobs until finally she is still. You never trust her enough to let go.

You are still in this position when you wake the next morning.

Turn to August 14, 2003

January 13, 2004

January 24, 2004

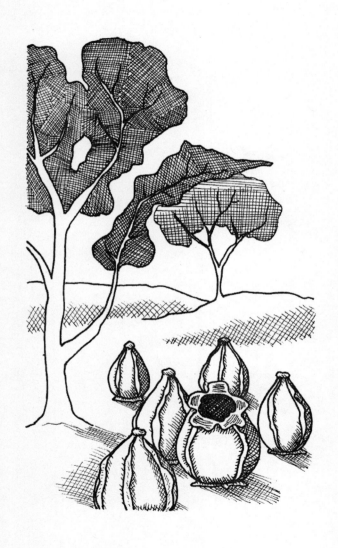

January 24, 2004

Anne is pregnant. On one hand, fuck.

On the other hand, one of the things you love about Anne is that there is never a question about whether or not she will want to get an abortion.

To wait and see what emerges from the pulsating egg, turn to September 29, 2003

If you decide to play it safe and use the torch to set fire to the nest before any more of the eggs show signs of life, turn to February 20, 2004

February 12, 2004

When you were young a teacher told you that every time you ripped a leaf off a tree or tore a flower from the ground, it was like putting another nail in Jesus on the cross. It made you wonder about the state of Jesus after all these years. Two thousand years is a lot of nails. How much damage can an immortal body stand? What sort of repercussions to the system do those thousands and thousands of nails have? If he has taken that many then it seems reasonable that there should be no limit to how many he can bear.

You have started to think of her drinking as something like tearing the leaves off trees: every time she goes and gets drunk it puts another nail into the crucified body of your relationship. None of them pierce vital organs but the number keeps building. You wonder what happens when there is nothing left. What happens when the body of the relationship is just nails all the way down?

Turn to March 6, 2006

February 20, 2004

Two hours before Anne is due to have an abortion she calls you into the bathroom. While she was taking a shower she miscarried. She asks if you want to check out the fetus. You give each other high fives, and then celebrate not having to spend the money for an abortion by going out and getting Indian buffet.

Turn to October 27, 2005

March 10, 2004

Your roommate has decided that her drinking is out of control and she needs to move back to Boston. You tell Anne that you are not going to keep this apartment and that she needs to find a new place to live. There is no question in your mind that it is not going to be with you. You tell her that if she wants this relationship to survive she can't live with you anymore.

Turn to September 2, 2003

April 19, 2004

Anne has her new apartment. It is the second floor of a huge house. Her bedroom window faces a Jewish elementary school. She likes to change in front of it, corrupting the young minds. Her place is huge, and cheap, and beautiful, and you are jealous of it. But you can't do it anymore. You need a place to retreat to when things get bad. If you can't have that there is no way this is going to survive.

Turn to May 28, 2003

June 11, 2004

11:00 pm. The phone rings and you answer.

"Hello?"
"Hi! Whatcha up to?!"
"I'm sleeping."
"Okay! I'm going to come over."
"Come over if you want, but I'm sleeping."
"That's fine! I am at a bar just down the street. I am going to find someone to give me a ride I'll see you in a bit!"

11:07. The phone rings.

"Hello?"
"Hi! I'm going to come over!"
"I know, you just called and told me that."
"I did?"
"Yeah. And I am trying to sleep."
"Okay I am going to come over then."
"That's fine, let yourself in, I am going to go back to sleep."
"Okay I will get a ride and be right over."

11:22. The phone rings.

"What is it?"
"What are you doing?"
"I am trying to sleep."
"Oh. Well I just wanted to let you know that I found a ride and I will be there in a few minutes."
"Fine. That's fine. I am going to go back to sleep now."

June 11, 2004

11:34. The phone rings.

"What."
"Hi, I am going to come over!"
"...."
"I thought I was going to get a ride from my friend but she is too drunk so I am just going to walk there."
"That is fine. I'm sleeping."
"Okay well I will be there in a few minutes and then we can hang out."
"No, you can come over, but I am sleeping."
"Okay well I will see you soon!"

11:38. The phone rings.

"What."
"Hi! Are you sleeping?"
"Yeah. What is it?"
"It's really cold out, I don't want to walk up there. My friend is going to give me a ride."
"That is fine, I don't care. Just come over and don't wake me up."
"Okay I'll be there in a few minutes!"

Turn to August 2, 2004

June 12, 2004

2:00 pm. The phone rings and you answer.

"Hello?"
"Hi! What are you doing?"
"What?! What happened last night?!"
"What do you mean?"
"You kept calling me when I was sleeping about how you were coming over and you never did!"
"No I didn't!"
"Yes you did! You called me five times last night!"
"Really?!"
"Yeah!"
"Shit! Cocaine is fucking amazing!"

Turn to August 11, 2005

July 10, 2004

Anne was drinking with her roommate and a friend. It was getting late, the friend was drunk, and they walked her home. They got to the friend's house and her roommates are hanging out on the porch. Anne says, "Here is your friend. Mind if I use your bathroom?" And for whatever reason, they did mind. Which yeah, is a dick thing to do, especially if you just walked their blind-drunk roommate home to make sure that she arrived safely. But that does not excuse pulling down your pants and pissing on their yard. And it especially does not excuse asking them to run inside and get you some toilet paper.

So the next day she is showing you the bruises on her arms, demonstrating an amazingly small amount of collateral damage considering she just fought five people. Maybe it is wishful thinking on your part, but it is times like these that make you wonder if your girlfriend isn't secretly a product of the Weapon X program.

Turn to October 4, 2003

August 2, 2004

Anne's apartment is kind of messy, and there is rarely food there, and nothing in the way of TV or video games or things like that. But that's not the reason you don't like to spend the night there. The reason you don't like to spend the night there is stuff like this:

"Hey, wake up!"

"Mmph... wha...?"

And that was the moment Anne dropped the snake on your face.

Turn to January 20, 2003

August 2, 2004

September 11, 2004

An e-mail, from Anne:

"So guess what I did. I got trashed on SundAY NIGHT ALL BY MYSELF and cracked my ribs in the street and have been in bed with poisoning unitl today (tues, 5 pm). I missed my first theory class, the signups for symphony so now I wait until next quarter, I called out of work, I cant breathe and i lost my Goddamn phone. It is no where to be found, it is dead, so it can't help us. I hate my stupid moronic self for doing such stupid things and it was worse earlier and only got better because i brushed my teeth. If you could come over and slip some arsenic into my bubble bath maybe I will slowly rot and then I can blame it on you. OKAY??"

Today would have marked two months of sobriety.

If you decide to kill yourself rather than risk being taken alive, turn to January 20, 2005

If you decide to take as many of the Ant-Warriors with you as you can and go down fighting, turn to December 23, 2004

September 27, 2004

Tonight, drunk, Anne and her roommate will drive down to Rite Aid to buy vodka. While there they will get into a fight and the roommate will walk home, leaving Anne in the parking lot. Anne will proceed to drink the bottle of vodka, then start threatening passersby until she is eventually arrested for drunk and disorderly. When she is released the next day, her car will still be there, parked illegally, doors open, cello and laptop still sitting inside. The only thing missing is her dog who has been taken to the pound. The dog she loves more than life itself. You would like to think that this would be enough to make her hit bottom.

You want to swear. You want to scream profanity with such rage that it causes plants to wither and pregnant women to miscarry. But that would be nothing. You swear all the time. Swearing is trite. Right now the hurt and the anger is so far beyond profanity. You know the drinking isn't about you or about the relationship. You know she is not destroying her life to spite you. She destroys her life because she is an alcoholic. You barely enter into the equation. That doesn't make it hurt any less.

You never imagined this as being a "forever" type of relationship. Anne is not a happily-ever-after kind of girl. You knew sooner or later Anne would break up with you while drunk, or she would do something so horrible you would snap and end it in one moment of righteous fury. But you are coming to realize that that moment is never going to arrive. You want to believe that things can be

September 27, 2004

better. That if she could leave the alcohol behind that she could be the one. No matter how bad it gets you just bend and bend and bend and there is no snapping.

You have a bad feeling about this.

If you decide to confront the Evil Power Master, turn to October 13, 2002

If you decide to wait and see what he does, turn to the next page

September 30, 2004

This is when it starts to get really awful. This is when Anne convinces herself that since her body can process a shot of vodka per hour, as long as she doesn't drink more than that she will never actually get drunk. This is the start of her doing a shot an hour, on the hour, pretty much every day for the next six months. During those six months there will be four, maybe five times that you will see her sober, and most of those are when you accompany her to court.

Turn to June 29, 2006

October 20, 2004

What do you owe someone you love? What do you owe someone who loves you? Anne has stopped taking her antidepressants. She says she doesn't like the way they make her feel. She doesn't like being numb to the world. She doesn't like how if affects her thinking or her music.

This is not the first time she has done this.

You know this is just going to make the drinking worse. She will get depressed, and she will drink, and she will be cruel. "This is the real me," she says, and you don't know what to do. How do you tell someone you don't want to be with them unless they medicate themselves into a happier version of who they think they really are? What right do you have to ask someone to take drugs to eliminate the parts of their personality that are inconvenient to you? What obligation do you have to put up with their abuse? Anne has had a hard life. She has legitimate reasons to be depressed. You ask yourself what kind of partner you are if you are not willing to help her with this burden.

If you try to pull the Ant-Warrior up onto the ledge, turn to October 19, 2003

If you let the Ant-Warrior fall to his death, turn to January 13, 2004

October 20, 2004

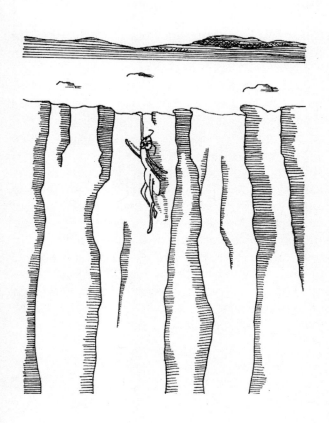

December 23, 2004

There is a scene towards the end of *Return of the Jedi* where Luke is dueling with Darth Vader and he totally loses it. The Alliance Fleet is doomed, Han and Leia have just walked into a trap, Palpatine is mocking him, and Luke starts wailing on Vader as hard as he can with his lightsaber. Just beating the fuck out of him. It is one of those perfect moments where years of frustration burst forth into pure transcendent rage.

You are having one of those moments now. You have always been scared of your own potential for anger. You have never let yourself get as bad as you are right now, but tonight was too much. Three months, and she is drunk every time you see her. Tonight was supposed to be different. A nice evening at the movies, and she promised she would be sober for it. She showed up stinking of vodka, and during the movie yelled at the screen. All you wanted was a night where she didn't try to ruin things. A night where she was just a normal person. Now you sit in the passenger seat of her car. Outside of your apartment. Her body reeking of alcohol as she sits next to you, silently watching, as you kick in the dashboard of her car.

Turn to May 12, 2003

January 2, 2005

Anne is with her family in North Carolina. An e-mail:

"I would also like to express to you again, of how all my sins have been purged for the coming new year. I spent 24 hours unable to drink any thing and puking and shitting and I am exhausted, but my brain is clearer than it has been in a while. Makes me uptight, but I kind of like it. I was just telling my sister today that every time I throw up, i miss you a little more."

Turn to November 26, 2002

January 20, 2005

You wake up to a phone call from Anne. She just posted bail after being arrested for kicking a cop in the balls. You're sure there is a great story behind this that undoubtedly involves heroic amounts of alcohol, but you just say that you'll talk to her later and stumble back to bed.

Turn to August 11, 2005

February 12, 2005

An e-mail, to Anne:

"I don't know if you can remember this, but I came over to your house a few weekends ago after you got out of work. i was coming over there to hang out and watch a movie, but when i got there you were drunk, so i talked to you about what the drinking was going to do to our relationship. i said i wasn't just going to break up with you because of it, and i knew i couldn't give you an ultimatium like "stop drinking or i'm going to leave you". but i told you then that as long as you were drinking we would almost never see or talk to each other. and, well, that's what's happening.

February 12, 2005

"i miss you too, and i promise you that for me it is much worse. cause in order for me to deal with this, i've had to split you into two people, sober anne and drinking anne. and i think i've seen sober anne four times since november; two of those were me accompanying you to court, and once to planned parenthood.

"so, yeah. the whole situation makes me really sad. i don't know whats going on anymore cause i can't even call you anymore without risking getting you when you've been drinking, and that just makes me feel worse. and the situation is really shitty, but its a situation we have chosen for ourselves: you choose to drink, and i choose to have a problem with your drinking, and for us i don't know if there is an alternative to this right now."

If you agree to fight the other prisoner to the death, turn to October 24, 2003

If you refuse to duel for the Ant-Warriors' amusement, turn to October 20, 2004

March 7, 2005

You are sitting in Anne's apartment listening to her demo. She recorded today for the first time. After the amount you have seen her struggle you can't help but smile to finally see her get closer to her dream. She asks you why you are smiling and you laugh. She accuses you of laughing at her and hating her music and she starts smacking you, which only makes you laugh harder.

Turn to September 2, 2005

March 30, 2005

You are helping Anne move out of her apartment. You are thinking to yourself that the move is going really smoothly, right up until the point when she tries to pull the shower curtain off the rod and ends up ripping the rail out of the ceiling, and then the next night gets so drunk that she is violently ill and she can't empty the apartment in time, and then the landlord stops by the apartment when she isn't home and sends her cats to the pound, and then gets kicked out of her new place after her roommate threatens to kill her, and then she ends up staying with you with her four cats until she can find a new apartment. But considering it's Anne it really could have gone much worse.

Turn to April 19, 2004

April 12, 2005

After thirty minutes of drunken insults and abuse, Anne is begging. She presses her body against you, pawing at your crotch. She pleads with you to stay, to fuck her. She says she feels so alone and that she needs you to stay and be with her and she presses her mouth against yours. You don't know what to do so you kiss her back and you hate it. You don't want to be here and you don't want to leave her alone.

She needs help. She needs so much help and she is like a black hole. You give and you give and you give and you give and you give and it makes no difference. You can spend the rest of your life feeding energy into her, and it will all be destroyed in the singularity of her alcoholism. She is entropy.

You push her away and she starts sobbing. She just wants to be close to you. She wants to feel you next to her and to know that you care and to know that you love her. She is terrified of being abandoned. You don't want to hurt her. Despite everything, you really don't want to cause the pain that leaving her like this would inflict. She is on her knees in front of you pulling weakly at your clothes when you turn around and reach for the door. She screams and it is horrible. It is sorrow and hopelessness and despair and the strength of it almost knocks you down, but you walk out the door and down the hall and she collapses to the ground like a skin discarded. She is still screaming as you step outside.

You tell yourself that she won't remember this.

April 12, 2005

The amount she drank tonight was far beyond blackout drunk. Whether you had stayed or left, it will make no difference to her tomorrow.

Turn to August 11, 2005

April 22, 2005

Reasons today is important:

1) You convince Anne to stop drinking, thus ending her six-and-a-half month long binge.
2) You take some time off work to help care for her while she goes through withdrawal. While discussing ways to keep her distracted during the process, she agrees to try watching that *Lost* show you've been talking about.

EVERYTHING'S COMING UP MILHOUSE.

If you tell the other captives to follow you into the cave of Ant-Warrior nutrient pools, turn to August 18, 2006

If you would rather have them follow you into the hall of discarded carapaces, turn to December 8, 2005

May 20, 2005

You are headed to Toronto with Anne and her mom and sister. This is your first time meeting her mom, and it explains so much. Seriously. It is enlightening, bordering on revelatory. Meeting Anne's mom is like the moment you find out that Kevin Spacey is actually Keyser Soze. The drinking. The speaking in riddles. The detached air that gives the impression that they can see a dimension that no one else can. The time her mom decided she wanted a convertible so she cut the roof off her car with a chainsaw. A personality that runs as a single thread through the center of both. Seeing them together, you can't imagine how they could end up being anyone but themselves.

Turn to March 30, 2003

July 12, 2005

You usually find yourself at a loss when trying to explain to others exactly how unexpectedly crazy Anne's life can be. It can be difficult to remember stories that would illustrate this that are not horrible and depressing. But today's event will be the go-to catastrophe for years to come.

Anne is driving around with her two dogs in the car. Both are still wearing leashes. It is a hot day, and she has the windows down. Out of the blue her Shih Tzu decides to make a break for it, and launches himself out the passenger side window. Anne lunges after him, and manages to grab his leash before he can hit the ground. So she has to drive the car with one hand while trying to pull her dog back into the car with the other.

That is a pretty good Anne story. That, multiplied by every single day that she is alive, is what it is like to be around her.

Turn to March 30, 2005

August 11, 2005

An email, to Anne:

So, I get the feeling you're not really taking the alcoholism thing seriously at the moment. The majority of the times I've talked to you over the past two weeks, you have either been drunk, or promising that you will now stop drinking, having gotten drunk the night before.

As we've discussed in the past, you are incapable of remembering how bad things get when you are at your worst. After a while of sobriety you usually lapse, not realizing how dire the consequences of your drinking can be. So, to aid you in your efforts for sobriety, I am going to give you some consequences. If you drink again between now and the end of the month, I will not go with you to North Carolina to meet your family. And if I find out you are drinking and hiding it from me, or you lie to me about drinking, it will be worse. I can assure you, it is better for me to be merely disappointed than actually angry.

If you decide to wrestle the Ant-Mummy back into the tomb, turn to April 5, 2006

If you decide to push the Ant-Mummy into the torch and set his wrappings on fire, turn to November 13, 2005

August 11, 2005

August 21, 2005

You are lying in bed with Anne. You are reading. She is not. You look over the top of your book to see her cleaning out her belly button. Somehow a dog hair got stuck in there (you are not sure why you are saying "somehow"; she has two dogs and four cats. The amazing thing is that there's only one hair). She tries to pluck it out but she has bitten her fingernails off, and it's buried too deep for her to grip it. So... jeez, just writing this makes my skin crawl... she places her fingers on either side of her navel and pushes in and down, until she forces her belly button inside out. Then with one hand pinches it at the base to hold it in position, and plucks the now-exposed hair out with the other. Ugh. Maybe this is a normal thing. Maybe this is something that everyone does and you just don't know about it. But damn, if it is, you don't want to know. This scene goes in the ever-expanding list of things that Anne does that are simultaneously disgusting but also sort of amazing.

Turn to March 30, 2003

September 2, 2005

Anne is driving the two of you down to North Carolina. It will be your first time meeting most of her family. It will be the first time you see where she comes from. It has Anne in a thoughtful mood. She asks, "Do you think we work as a couple?" You smile and turn to her and say, "Yeah, I think we work really well as a couple. We counterbalance each other. You are a passionate free spirit who brings adventure and excitement into my otherwise boring existence. And I try to stop you. Everybody wins."

She scowls at you. You kiss her cheek in response.

Turn to May 20, 2005

September 20, 2005

You think to yourself there is a point where it is no longer worthwhile to stay. Your friends are the main thing keeping you here, and they are scattering to the winds at an increasing pace.

Today your best friend tells you he is moving to San Francisco. You realize how close to the tipping point you have come. Finding a new place to live with a better music scene is something that you and Anne have talked about before, but today is the first time you talk about it in earnest. This is the first day of you moving to Portland.

Turn to August 14, 2003

October 27, 2005

A man asks you a question:

"So, do you have kids?"
"Nope."
"Married?"
"Nope."
"Girlfriend?"
"Yep."
"What does she do?"
"She's a cellist."
"Oh dear god. I feel for you man. Nothing in the world harder than dating a cellist. Holy shit, that'll kill ya."

Turn to December 7, 2002

November 13, 2005

Today is your birthday, and it is one of the worst experiences of your life. This whole weekend has been so fucking horrible and frustrating and stupid and pointless. You will never again speak about what happened this weekend. You are certainly not going to talk about it now. This is the last time you will try to celebrate your birthday.

Turn to October 6, 2006

December 8, 2005

In retrospect, taking a vacation in New Orleans three months after Hurricane Katrina might have been a bad idea. You saw the news stories about schools reopening and people coming home and were fooled into thinking that the city had returned to some semblance of normalcy. It is four in the morning and you are completely lost. It is dark. There is no power and there are no lights and you are driving through the garbage-clogged streets of abandoned neighborhoods hoping to find a gas station before the car hits empty. You are trying very hard to be more excited than scared. You are grateful that Anne is with you. You are grateful that you have a girlfriend who agrees that this is an adventure, and not a horrible mistake.

Turn to February 13, 2006

January 10, 2006

Anne has been sober for about a week. You used to hear people say that they had been sober for a week, or a month, or a year, or whatever, and it didn't really mean anything to you. A week does not seem like a very long time if you aren't an addict. But after the last three years you have come to appreciate how much of an accomplishment seven days can be.

Turn to July 14, 2006

February 13, 2006

You have never been as proud of Anne as you are right now. More than getting into music school. More than watching her orchestra. More than attending her recitals. More than hearing her first recordings. More than seeing her play live with her band. More than having five dollars to her name and seeing her give it to a homeless person. More than driving through the mountains at night on icy roads in a blizzard. More than hearing that it took six people to take her down in a fight. Because today is the day that, after weeks of trying, she will finally finish *Super Mario World*.

Turn to June 9, 2006

March 6, 2006

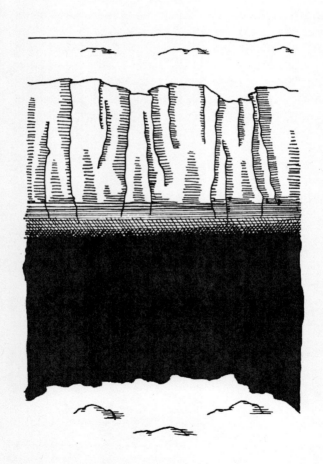

March 6, 2006

You assumed that you would be getting separate apartments after you got to Portland. With the exception of those four months she crashed in your apartment after leaving music school you've never lived together. But today Anne tells you that she is worried about having enough money once she gets there and she wants the two of you to get a place together. This worries you. A lot. The two of you are doing well at the moment: Anne has been sober for about two months and your relationship feels as solid as it's ever been. But the thing that has always made her drinking tolerable in the past is the ability to go to your own apartment and not see her for a week when things turn bad.

You know she needs this. But you can't help but feel that if you agree you are dooming the relationship in the process.

If you jump across the chasm, turn April 26, 2006

If you decide to turn back and look for another way around, turn to June 29, 2003

April 5, 2006

This feels like a vacation. You quit your job, you broke your lease, and for the next month you are living with Anne in her tiny apartment. Everything you own is packed in boxes, stacked against the wall, except for your computer and a box of clothes. Anne is sober, you eat pizza and Indian food all the time, your nights are spent playing video games while Anne sits next to you practicing the cello. Your life resembles the state of relaxed, responsibility-free bliss you only hear about in Disney songs sung by warthogs or bears. You feel really good about this.

To hell with it. You tell Anne you will get a place with her after you get to Portland. You are going to have to move in together sooner or later. It's not like waiting another three and a half years is going to make you more ready than you already are. And honestly, if you can't live together without breaking up, you would rather find that out now than ten years down the road.

Turn to February 12, 2004

April 5, 2006

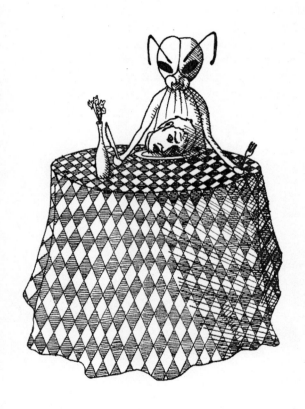

April 10, 2006

Today is Anne's first real concert. Not playing in some coffeehouse, but in an actual club. Right now she is on the stage where you saw The White Stripes and Sufjan Stevens and Wesley Willis and Xiu Xiu and Dresden Dolls and Modest Mouse and a hundred other indie rock nobodies who would one day achieve some modicum of notoriety. You watch her attack her cello, and daydream about what it will be like to be a rock star's wife. Playing video games all day, sleeping on a giant pile of money all night. Yeah. Someday this will all be worth it.

Turn to September 10, 2002

April 26, 2006

You have never considered yourself to be that good at Tetris, but after three days of trying you have finally managed to fill the trailer with an orderly precision that would make Alexey Pazhitnov proud. You slide the door closed, bolt the latch shut, and climb into Anne's Jeep.

Up until a month ago you did not know how to drive a car. But this is a three thousand mile trip and you are sharing the Jeep with Anne, her three cats, her Shih Tzu, and her Great Dane. You will be damned if you are going to spend one second longer in this car than you need to. So, now you know how to drive. You don't have your license or anything, but you know enough to go in a straight line down a highway at 65 miles an hour.

The trip goes smoother than you could have possibly dreamed. Yes, you get a flat tire in the badlands of Wyoming. Yes, when a truck driver stops to help you out the Shih Tzu gets so upset that he poops in the box of coins you had been using for tolls. But the drive is peaceful, the scenery more breathtaking than the grasslands and valleys and mountains of Azeroth, and three days later you are in your new home.

Turn to September 16, 2006

June 9, 2006

Portland is wonderful. You don't have a job yet, but that's fine. You and Anne fill your days watching movies and going to shows and playing video games and buying the ugliest furniture you can find and then spray painting it an even uglier color. Anne finds a drummer and a record label and starts playing house shows and finishing work on her album. You lower your guard. As worried as you were about all of this, it really feels like it is going to be okay.

If you decide to create a distraction so the rest of the group can slip by the Ant-Warriors guarding the tunnel entrance, turn to March 2, 2003

If you decide to take Captain Lyra up on her offer to provide the distraction while you and the others escape to freedom, turn to March 7, 2005

June 20, 2006

Anne has started drinking again. When you moved to Portland you told everyone that you met —her drummer, her new friends, the guy who ran her label— that she absolutely couldn't drink. Both of you sat with those people and explained that Anne is unable to make intelligent decisions about alcohol. That it is a destructive influence in her life and that they must never encourage her to drink or tell her that it's okay for her to drink. That giving Anne alcohol is like getting her wet, feeding her after midnight, and exposing her to bright lights all rolled up in one.

They betrayed your trust. They bought her drinks because they wanted to see her drunk, or get into her pants, or for other stupid, shortsighted reasons that each of them will come to regret within the year. Anne is trying to hide it from you but you know it's all starting again. It's been a good six months.

If you decide to shoot the traitors, turn to December 19, 2002

If you decide to walk away and leave them to their fate, turn to July 29, 2006

July 14, 2006

When Anne left she promised that she wouldn't be drinking. She said that she and her drummer were just getting together to talk about some stuff for the show the next day. But she wouldn't drink, and she would make sure that her drummer wouldn't drink so she wouldn't be tempted.

You don't know if she meant that or not. If she really intended to stay sober, or if she was just saying that hoping that she wouldn't get caught. You suppose in the scheme of things it doesn't really matter. She broke her promise. She got drunk and the drummer got drunk. The drummer drove them home in her car. On the way back from the practice space they got pulled over. Somehow the cops didn't give the drummer a breathalyzer. Somehow they didn't realize that the drummer was driving on a suspended license due to a previous DUI. All they did was take the car and tell Anne she would have to pick it up in the morning.

It is four in the morning when she finally gets in. At the sight of her home safe there is a minuscule flicker of relief amongst an inferno of anger. After everything you have done for her. After all the bullshit you put up with and all the help you give her and all the patience and all the time and every fucking drop of energy in your soul to help her be okay. How fucking dare she. She could have lost her drummer. She could have lost her car. You know you are being callous, you know you should just be happy she's safe, but she owes you. You want to see a return on your invest-

July 14, 2006

ment. How dare she jeopardize everything you have done for a bottle of cheap fucking vodka.

You are sitting on the couch in the living room in the dark. She is standing in the doorway to the kitchen. The kitchen light is on and as her silhouette explains what happened tonight and begs your forgiveness your heart begins to close. You cannot take this any more. If you need to be cold to protect yourself, then so be it.

It will be a week before you can stand to have her touch you again.

To succumb to the evil Ant-Demon that guards the tomb, turn to May 12, 2003

To try and resist its psychic attack, turn to October 3, 2006

July 29, 2006

You come home from work to discover Anne's car parked sideways in the driveway. Inside, she is still asleep, sprawled across the bed. You are not ready to deal with this yet. You make some oatmeal, you go upstairs, you read the news and try to find the calm within you that will allow you to ask what happened so that the words are a question and not an accusation. You walk back downstairs, climb into bed, shake her shoulder to wake her up.

It was her friend, she claims. Her friend drove them here in her car and then the friend took a cab home. You ask her if they had been drinking; she says no. You ask her why, if they weren't drunk, they parked the car sideways. She says they didn't, that she doesn't know what you are talking about. You tell her in the driveway her car is parked sideways. She says it isn't. You ask her to come outside. The sun is high and bright. The asphalt is hot under your bare feet, and Anne stares at the car, blinking at the assault of the light against her eyes. You are looking at her, and she is looking at the car, and neither of you have anything to say.

Turn to May 14, 2003

August 7, 2006

You ask Anne to limit herself to beer. To not drink alone. To not bring alcohol into the house. But no. You go to work, she walks down the street to the liquor store and brings home a bottle of vodka. Eight hours after she agreed to these rules so that hopefully she wouldn't spiral out of control so fast that the relationship couldn't be saved, she breaks her promise. You knew you couldn't really count on Anne to keep her word when things got bad. But today wasn't bad. It was just another day. And still she couldn't give you eight hours. Eight fucking hours. Four years you've been together, and you trust her less now than when you first met.

Turn to September 27, 2004

August 18, 2006

Anne is drunk and you need to get out of the house. She is not supposed to be in your room when she is drinking but she is here anyway, belligerent and screaming and sobbing. You can't deal with this. You need to go. You leave her in your room and run down the stairs and start looking for your shoes. There is a Safeway a few blocks away that is open 24 hours. You can spend the night there if you need to. You are in the kitchen when you hear a rapid thumping from the stairs that can only be the sound of Anne falling.

You put your head in your hands. You were so close to being out the door. Another thirty seconds was all you needed. Another thirty seconds and you wouldn't have to deal with whatever comes next.

Anne is lying on the floor at the base of the stairs. Her eyes are closed and she is not moving. You say her name and she doesn't respond. You move closer. You can see now that she is not breathing. Her jaw is clenched tight and there is a murky white liquid streaming out of her nose, covering her face. There is no blood. She still is not moving.

You don't want to touch her. This feels like a trap. She is drunk and she is vicious and she will do anything to hurt you right now and the second you put your hands near her face she is going to snap awake and bite your fingers off. This is a trap. This is a trap and if you try to touch her you are going to lose a hand but you have no choice

August 18, 2006

because she is still not breathing and if you don't help her she is going to die.

You slap her face. Lightly, gingerly. She doesn't respond. You do it harder. And again. And she is still not moving, still not breathing. This is a trap. She is a snake and you need to open her mouth and the second you touch her lips she is going to bite off your finger. You do it anyway. You pull her lips apart and force your nails between her teeth and it is all you can do to pry her jaw open and as you do vomit spills from her mouth out onto the floor. You swab your fingers inside her mouth to clear it of liquid but she is still quiet.

You grab her under the shoulders and you wrestle her dead weight into the bathroom and over the lip of the tub into the nutrient pool of the Ant-Warriors. Her body slowly sinks down into the luminescent slime until only her head remains above the surface. You turn the cold water tap as far as it will go and as the spray of the shower hits her she finally begins to rouse. She looks around the cavern, faintly glowing pools stretching off as far as she can see, and asks, "Where am I? What happened?"

Turn to October 7, 2006

September 14, 2006

Much in the same way that you would not be cool with meth addicts stealing your bike because they need money to get a fix, you are also not cool with Anne's Great Dane creating giant watery piles of shit all over the bedroom rug, then walking in them, then pulling the comforter off the bed so she can lie on it. Both are instances where a creature is acting as a slave to their biological functions in a way that fucks with your property. You know that Anne feels the exact opposite about this issue, that the consequences of actions should be forgiven if they are the result of biological imperatives and predispositions. But maybe you are insensitive because that excuse has been used on you a few too many times.

Turn to December 17, 2003

September 16, 2006

You share a house with Anne, and that is all. You look at her and you talk to her and you feel nothing. The part of you that loves her has turned to ash. You know it will come back. You have done this before. You just need to keep your head down and push forward and as long as things stay stable eventually all this will fade.

Right now you are talking to her and you can't hide the lack of warmth in your voice. You wish you could. You want to act like everything is normal until it becomes true again. But it is not in you anymore. She looks at you and in every conversation her eyes are nothing but sorrow because she knows she did this to you.

Today you buy a CD. You take out the liner notes and look at the lyrics and read "Loneliness isn't being alone, it's when someone loves you and you don't have it in you to love them back," and you want to collapse under the weight of those words.

If you fall to the ground, turn to October 30, 2006

If you ambush the Ant-Warriors as they enter the cave, turn to October 6, 2006

October 3, 2006

You had a good weekend. You went to Massachusetts to be a groomsman in your friends' wedding. For their post-ceremony music, instead of playing *The Wedding March* they played the theme from *Final Fantasy*. You got to see a lot of friends who you hadn't seen since moving to Portland. You feel refreshed.

Anne picks you up at the airport. The two of you drive around putting up flyers then go home and watch *Arrested Development* and for the first time in a month at the end of the night you climb into bed next to her.

Turn to June 12, 2004

October 6, 2006

An e-mail, to Anne:

So, was it not just last week that I told you "I can deal with the alcoholism. I can deal with being lonely all the time. I don't like it, but oh well. Just don't break my heart again. For once, tell me the truth on whether you are really going to stop drinking this time. Because I am tired of being alone, but it is still so much better than getting my hopes up only to be betrayed by you again. I will be okay as long as I can keep myself closed up, guarded. Just please don't let me start to trust you again if you are not serious.

Did I not say that seven days ago?

Seriously, why the fuck would you do that? Is it stupidity or selfishness? You had your fucking sponsor at the club with you, so I'm assuming you had at least one person reminding you of how you shouldn't be drinking. And yet you do it anyways.

Turn to November 13, 2002

October 7, 2006

An e-mail, from Anne:

I was just sitting down to write you an email. I wanted to ask about all of the Pain in your eyes when I saw you upstairs. Briefly. You are dripping with it.

Then I got your email. And that explained what I already knew to be the case. Its funny how I forget so much that my drinking cause you a deep pain. I hate it when you are in a shell and very distant. Something that I have told you time and time again, that doesn't really make a difference, is that I would never do anything to put pain in your eyes. Never. I was so happy when I thought, 2 weeks ago, that surely I could quit...this time. Surely. That was enforced when you crawled up in bed with me, and I saw my old you. Not the distant,, cold, angry, lonely you. Please understand that I am . With my heart. Trying to figure out how to live without alcohol. Alcoholism, is something that can't be understood without actually being an alcoholic. The best thing I can think of, is a starving man. Starving to death in front of a buffett. He will be able to hold off from eating for only so long. He will be come obsessed with the food on my plate.

This is why it is hard for me to find an answer to your question of why the fuck I drank. The absolute joy of having you in my arms, as an untroubled person, was incredible. I found, peace. I am not sure if any happiness is stronger than my addiction. That is what it is. I realize we have been

October 7, 2006

struggling with this for a while. I don't think you can grasp what that is. ITs not stupidity. Its not selfishness. It is a disease.

I am going to play music now. It helps me feel okay. I have had a good cry and now I will sing. I miss you. Please know. I am trying with all of my heart to be broken enough somewhere inside, so that I can quit. I always start off broken, then when I feel better, I think I might be okay this time. I grew up in aa. I know all of the slogans and recommendations. I have alot of knowledge. What I don't have, is that moment that you give up. Do what they tell you to do. Give it up to a higher power, do a personal inventory, write out all of your resentments.....Stuff. Call people,. make coffee.

I am working on it.

I miss you.

Turn to January 10, 2006

October 11, 2006

You are not worried about losing Anne. You are worried about losing the person she has the potential to be. She is amazing under all those layers of alcoholic. You don't want to give up on her and spend the rest of your life regretting having lost someone as unique as her. But you also don't want to spend the rest of your life waiting for her to change.

You ask yourself if you could be with her forever, and you tell yourself the answer is no. It has nothing to do with commitment. It has to do with being with a person who in their heart has a bottomless well of sorrow. Maybe you could turn things around. Maybe you could open up to her completely. Maybe if you could love her unconditionally with no regard for how much she hurt you, that might heal her wound. You dread that path. You look down it and see nothing except alcohol and disappointment and being trapped on this accursed planet until the day you die.

But you don't have to be with her for the rest of your life. You just have to be with her for today. Make it through today and go through all this again tomorrow. It doesn't feel like a prison if it's one day at a time.

If you shoot your way past the giant Ant-Warriors, turn to July 10, 2004

If you drop your blaster to the ground and raise your arms in surrender, turn to January 2, 2005

October 11, 2006

October 14, 2006

Anne is gone for a few weeks on tour. She is bringing her Ant-Warrior with her to help her sell merch. The Ant-Warrior who a week earlier admitted that he was in love with her. You think this is a bad idea, but Anne is convinced that something worse will happen if she has to deal with the drummer by herself for that long. She assures you that there is nothing to worry about. You trust her not to do anything, but you do not trust him. You can feel her slipping away.

Turn to July 14, 2006

October 30, 2006

Anne is back. Things are awkward. You missed her, and you are glad to see her again, but a particularly nasty looking Ant-Warrior is standing just a few feet away. You are safe behind this rock for now but sooner or later you are going to need to act. Anne tells you that she is going up to Seattle for a few days to work on stuff with her drummer and her merch guy and you don't know what to think. Maybe if you were to distract the Ant-Warrior in some way you could ambush him, or make a dash for the dimly lit tunnel to the south without him noticing. There is so much distance between you now. There are times when you will lie in bed together and you will read and she will play video games and this is as much as you have ever wanted. But there is something missing. You know you can't go on like this. You know that sooner or later the Ant-Warrior is going to look behind this rock. You need to do something and that terrifies you, because more than any other time over the past four years you are scared of what might happen next.

If you decide to attack the Ant-Warrior while his back is turned, turn to November 13, 2006

If you decide to start over, turn to November 13, 2006

November 13, 2006

As the Ant-Warrior guard falls dead at your feet, you look at the energy meter of your laser blaster. It is almost empty, but it will be enough. It has to be enough. You start to walk.

You are getting cold. You look down at your arm. A dark crimson stain has spread the length of the sleeve. It is numb. You tell your arm to move, and it moves, but it feels alien to you. Like it belongs to somebody else. Your entire body is beginning to feel stiff. The Ant-Warrior's toxin is spreading.

You force one foot in front of the other. Your legs are dead slabs of meat under your body. You think of the path behind you. There must be miles of tunnels. You are long past the point where you could go back. You contemplate everything that has happened to you, every choice you made, and you realize there was no possible outcome besides the one in front of you now. The warm steel of the blaster feels good in your hand. You stumble forward. The lair of the ant-queen is just a few yards away now. One way or another this will be the end of your story.

Turn to November 14, 2006

November 13, 2006

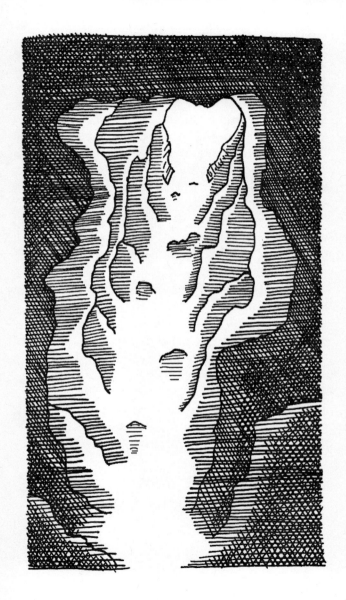

November 14, 2006

An e-mail, from Anne:

okay. this is bigger than my heart can hold. This is killing me.

I think we need to break up. Yooou don't feel like my boyfriend anymore.

I have been trying to avoid hurting you, but it has been happening anyway.

Please know that this breaks my heart. I love you. But it doesn't feel like the kind of love that is supposed to be between boyfriend and girlfriend.

I don't know that if in response to your walls, which I forced upon you, that I built my own. I don't think you have ever been passionate about me, and I have wanted that. I have been obsessed with what to say to you. You being precious to me. One of the

most precious things I have ever had. I do love you. Please know that. I don't know what to do from here. But I know that you deserve the truth and much more. So much more. This was not my intention. I never saw this coming. We have felt like roommates for some time now. That is not your fault, just what had to be done. But I can't turn this back into more than that.

The End

Epilogue

April 1, 2008

This is the day that Anne has her last drink.

ABOUT THE AUTHOR AND ILLUSTRATOR

The author continues to live in Portland, Oregon. This is his first Not a Choose Your Own Adventure book.

Sarah Miller is a graduate of the College of Creative Studies at UC Santa Barbara. Something of a bricoleuse, Ms. Miller likes to try her hand at a broad range of art forms. This is her first work as an illustrator. Other examples of her art can be viewed at www.theinvisibleocean.com.